Oklahoma

BY M. J. YORK

Published by The Child's World®
1980 Lookout Drive • Mankato, MN 56003-1705
800-599-READ • www.childsworld.com

ACKNOWLEDGMENTS
The Child's World®: Mary Berendes, Publishing Director
The Design Lab: Design and production
Red Line Editorial: Editorial direction

PHOTO CREDITS: Karen Harrison/iStockphoto, cover, 1, 3; Matt Kania/Map
Hero, Inc., 4, 5; Chris Pritchard/iStockphoto, 7; David Parsons/iStockphoto,
9; iStockphoto, 10; Mia Blake/iStockphoto, 11; Pattie Calfy/iStockphoto, 13;
Nativestock Pictures/Photolibrary, 15; Allen Russell/Photolibrary, 17; Tony
Barton/AP Images, 19; Eric Foltz/iStockphoto, 21; One Mile Up, 22; Quarter-
dollar coin image from the United States Mint, 22

LIBRARY OF CONGRESS CATALOGING-IN-PUBLICATION DATA
York, M. J., 1983–
  Oklahoma / by M.J. YorK.
      p. cm.
  Includes bibliographical references and index.
  ISBN 978-1-60253-480-3 (library bound : alk. paper)
  1. Oklahoma—Juvenile literature. I. Title.

F694.3.Y67 2010
976.6–dc22

2010019310

Printed in the United States of America in Mankato, Minnesota.
July 2010
F11538

On the cover:
Oklahoma has
many farms.

CONTENTS

4 Geography

6 Cities

8 Land

10 Plants and Animals

12 People and Work

14 History

16 Ways of Life

18 Famous People

20 Famous Places

22 *State Symbols*

23 *Glossary*

24 *Further Information*

24 *Index*

Geography

Let's explore Oklahoma! Oklahoma is in the middle of the United States.

COLORADO

KANSAS

MISSOURI

Guymon •

Ponca City •

Bartlesville •

Arkansas River

Pawnee •

OKLAHOMA

Tulsa •

Tahlequah •

Oklahoma City

Checotah •

Clinton •

Yukon •

Norman •

Anadarko •

Wichita
Mountains • Lawton

• Sulphur

Chickasaw
National
Recreation Area

Red River

ARKANSAS

Oklahoma is shaped
like a frying pan. The
thin part is called
the panhandle.

TEXAS

NORTH
WEST EAST
SOUTH

Cities

Oklahoma City is the capital of Oklahoma. It is also the largest city in the state. Tulsa and Norman are other well-known cities.

More than 500,000 people live in Oklahoma City. ▶

Land

Large parts of Oklahoma are **plains** and low hills. Larger hills and some small mountains are in the east. The Arkansas River flows through Oklahoma. The Red River is the state's southern border.

Oklahoma has some small mountains, but much of the land is flat. ▶

Plants and Animals

The state animal of Oklahoma is the bison. It is a large, brown animal with small horns. Bison roam the state's **prairies**. The scissor-tailed flycatcher is the state bird. It lives on prairies, too. The redbud is the state tree. It is small and has beautiful pink flowers. The state flower is the Oklahoma rose.

The redbud has flowers that open up in spring. ▶

People and Work

More than 3.6 million people live in Oklahoma. Farming, **ranching**, oil drilling, and mining are important in the state. Many people work in **manufacturing**. They make machines and **technology** for airplanes, spacecraft, and weather **research**.

Many ranchers in Oklahoma raise cattle. ▶

History

Native Americans have lived in the Oklahoma area for thousands of years. The United States bought the land in 1803 as part of the Louisiana Purchase. In the early 1800s, the government made Native American groups move from eastern states into the Oklahoma area. Other settlers were not allowed to live here at first. In 1889, other settlers were allowed to move in. Oklahoma became the forty-sixth state on November 16, 1907.

A group of Pawnee men wear beads and blankets. ▶

Oklahoma is called "the Sooner State." This is because some settlers moved in "sooner" than they were supposed to.

15

Ways of Life

Many Native Americans still live in Oklahoma. Their ways of life can be seen in the art, food, and beliefs of many people in the state. Oklahoma is also known for **cowboys** and its Wild West history.

A girl prepares a horse for a show in Weatherford, Oklahoma. ▶

Famous People

Country singers Reba McEntire, Toby Keith, Garth Brooks, and Carrie Underwood were born in Oklahoma. Actor Brad Pitt and baseball player Mickey Mantle were born in the state, too.

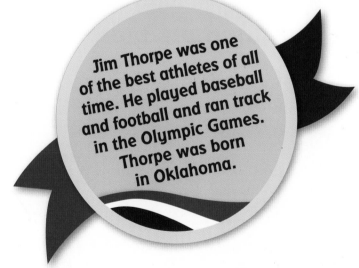

Jim Thorpe was one of the best athletes of all time. He played baseball and football and ran track in the Olympic Games. Thorpe was born in Oklahoma.

Singer Carrie Underwood grew up in Checotah, Oklahoma. ▶

Famous Places

People visit Chickasaw National **Recreation** Area. Chickasaw has beautiful streams and lakes. People drive through the state on **Route** 66. It is one of the most famous roads in the United States.

Travertine Creek is part of Chickasaw National Recreation Area in Oklahoma. ▶

State Symbols

Seal

Oklahoma's state seal has a large star in the center. In each arm of the star is a picture that stands for a Native American group. Go to childsworld.com/links for a link to Oklahoma's state Web site, where you can get a firsthand look at the state seal.

OKLAHOMA

Flag

The state flag shows a Native American peace pipe. It also has an olive branch, which stands for peace.

Quarter

Oklahoma's state quarter shows the state bird and the state wildflower, the Indian blanket. These stand for the state's natural beauty. The quarter came out in 2008.

Glossary

cowboys (KOW-boyz): Cowboys are men who take care of cattle or horses. Oklahoma is known for its cowboys.

manufacturing (man-yuh-FAK-chur-ing): Manufacturing is the task of making items with machines. Many people in Oklahoma work in manufacturing.

plains (PLAYNZ): Plains are areas of flat land that do not have many trees. Much of Oklahoma's land is plains.

prairies (PRAYR-eez): Prairies are flat or hilly grasslands. Bison live on Oklahoma's prairies.

ranching (RANCH-ing): Ranching is raising cattle or other large animals. Some people in Oklahoma work in ranching.

recreation (rek-ree-AY-shun): Recreation is the hobbies or other fun activities people enjoy during their spare time. Many visitors come to a large recreation area in Oklahoma.

research (REE-surch): Research is studying or experimenting on something. Machines for weather research are made in Oklahoma.

route (ROOT): A route is a path or road. Route 66 goes through Oklahoma.

seal (SEEL): A seal is a symbol a state uses for government business. Oklahoma's seal shows a star.

symbols (SIM-bulz): Symbols are pictures or things that stand for something else. The seal and flag are Oklahoma's symbols.

technology (tek-NAWL-uh-jee): Technology is scientific knowledge applied to practical things. Technology for airplanes, spacecraft, and weather research is made in Oklahoma.

Further Information

Books

Keller, Laurie. *The Scrambled States of America*. New York: Henry Holt, 2002.

Labella, Susan. *Oklahoma*. New York: Children's Press, 2007.

Scillian, Devin. *S is for Sooner: An Oklahoma Alphabet*. Chelsea, MI: Sleeping Bear Press, 2003.

Web Sites

Visit our Web site for links about Oklahoma: *childsworld.com/links*

Note to Parents, Teachers, and Librarians: We routinely verify our Web links to make sure they are safe and active sites. So encourage your readers to check them out!

Index

Arkansas River, 8

capital, 6
Chickasaw National Recreation Area, 20

jobs, 12

Native Americans, 14, 16

population, 12

Red River, 8
Route 66, 20

settlers, 14, 15

state animal, 10
state bird, 10
state flower, 10
state tree, 10

tourism, 20